HOW TO SET & ACHIEVE GOALS
for Kids

IT'S NEVER TOO EARLY TO SHINE

Kosi Eneli

9 year old author and avid reader

KANELI INTERNATIONAL INC.
PRESS

HOW TO SET & ACHIEVE GOALS FOR KIDS
PUBLISHED BY KANELI PRESS
P.O. Box 2789
Harker Heights, TX 76548

ISBN 978-0-9887516-0-6

Copyright © 2012 by Kosi Eneli

Book Design by Craig Creasy

Photography by Bethany Carpio

Printed in the United States of America
2012 – First Trade Paperback Edition

To my dear Mom who always believes in me, and my wonderful Dad who is such a great provider for our family. You both make it possible for me to live my dreams. I give you my greatest love.

CONTENTS

ACKNOWLEDGEMENTS

First of all, I want to thank my mother who made all of this possible. She encouraged me to put my thoughts on goals into a book. My dream had been to get a book published in the year 2012, but my fiction book requires illustrations and I wouldn't have been able to complete the whole process before the end of 2012. So, I came up with a different book. She gave up earning money from her coaching calls that help people to assist me. My mother is such a wonderful person that she used that time to make my dream come true.

I want to thank my Dad. He works long hours saving people's lives in the hospital. His hard work allows us to live comfortably and to enjoy a lot of experiences. He paid for the pictures for my book too. I love them both so much for helping me to make my dream come true. Thank you, Mommy and Daddy.

I also want to thank my aunts Somiari Demm, Titi Osu, cousin Dr. Ruth Molokwu and all my teachers and principal for encouraging me. There has been a particular teacher that throughout my journey has encouraged me and even promised to buy copies of my book, whom I must thank. When I walked through the school hallways sometimes believing I couldn't get it published, she was there to lift my spirits. Thank you, Mrs. Jennie Johnson, for your encouragement and support.

Natalie Creasy thanks for helping to edit my book. And thanks to Bethany Carpio for the great photo shoot. Thanks to my brothers and sister for letting me use the computer when I needed it. Finally, thanks to God for all his blessings.

What are Goals and Why are they Important?

What is a goal?

The definition of a goal that has been easiest for me to understand is, "A goal is simply a dream with a deadline." We all have dreams. Some of us may dream of going to Disney World or maybe you are just dreaming of getting the latest video game, or maybe you dream of being a teacher or a doctor someday. It is important to always have a dream in your heart. It gives meaning to your life.

A goal is a dream with a DEADLINE.

So, let's say you tell yourself, "Someday, I will get a scholarship for college." Well, because you did not specify when that day will be, it is not a goal, but rather it is a dream. Your goals must have a specific time by when you will achieve them. But, if instead you say, "I will make all A's this school year and start to prove that I am worthy of a college scholarship," now, that dream becomes a goal.

Let me share some more examples:

Dream: I would like to attend the principal's special party for students who read at least one book a week.
Goal: I will read at least one book every week for the entire school year so I qualify to attend the special party.

Dream: I would love to buy the latest video game.
Goal: I will do my chores daily and ask for more work so I can earn $30 to buy my video game by the summer.

All you need to create a goal is to know what you want and know exactly how much time you have to achieve it. If there is no specific time, it is not a goal.

It is important that you understand the difference between dreams and goals or you will never be as successful as you want to be. If you don't understand the difference, read over my examples again till you get it. Because a goal has a specific deadline, this causes you to be more focused about creating and following a plan to achieve your goal. Goals make you more focused.

Why are goals important?

I am so excited about teaching kids to set goals because setting and achieving goals is the path to a great life. All of us want a great life. We want nice things. We like getting rewarded. We don't want to be unhappy and miserable about our lives.

Every person you see who is successful had to set goals. I remember watching a show about Oprah Winfrey and she said she decided at a young age to be a good student and be successful. Now, she has her own TV network and has a school for girls in South Africa. I bet she had to set goals to do those things and still does.

Olympic gold medalist, Gabby Douglas set a goal too. Her goal was to train and do her best in the Olympics. As we all know, she won gold medals in both the individual and team all-around competitions.

In an interview, Gabby Douglas said, "I just want people to know it took a lot." It took a lot of hard days in the gym and determination, passion and drive. Gold medals are made out of your sweat, blood and tears, and effort in the gym every day, and sacrificing a lot that you have to do."

Today, Gabby Douglas is living her dream. She has been on magazine covers, is in the record books, has commercials, is on TV shows and is selling out arenas all over the country. It took goals to create the amazing life she is living.

Michael Phelps set some goals too and now he has more Olympic medals than anyone else. This is because he set goals to train and do his best. As of now, he has the most Olympic medals of anyone. He is a multi-millionaire and is also on TV shows and commercials.

My dad set a goal to be a physician and he is a respected physician today. I set a goal for myself to write and publish my first book before I turn 10 years old in 2013, and here you are reading my very first book. I met my goal.

Goals allow you to figure out where you want to go. If you don't know where you want to go, you may take the wrong road and get lost. In my opinion, you start with small goals and achieving that goal may help you become more successful. Then, as you get better and build more confidence, you set bigger goals.

Goals will make you stronger and more capable. Goals will build your self-confidence and self-esteem. Why? Because when you achieve something, you feel good about yourself, right? The better you feel about yourself, the better you will feel about your ability to have a successful life.

Some of you may be thinking, "Oh, I don't really need goals until I am an adult." Well, that's not true at all. Smart kids, like me, set goals. Setting goals and achieving them will keep you focused on growing and improving yourself. When you set and achieve goals, you may get promoted for something you really want like being asked to be on a team or nominated to participate in a special program. Here is an example:

My Goal: To have all A's, good attendance, and a good reputation the whole school year.

Actions: I paid attention and completed all work on time, was at school every day, stayed out of trouble, and took every opportunity to do my best.

Results: I earned all A Honor Roll and was selected to be a part of Nolanville Elementary School Television (NESTV).

I had dreamed of being a part of NESTV since first grade. NESTV is my school's television station and a select group of 4th and 5th graders are trained to deliver the news, weather, sports, and announcements on our school's television station as well as create scripts and work the cameras.

Interested students must submit a paragraph about why they should be selected for NESTV. Apparently, not only was my paragraph strong, the teachers and principal had spoken highly of me and I was given the opportunity to serve on NESTV. I am 1 of 10 students currently serving on NESTV and the only 4th grade girl.

As you can see, setting my goal to be a great student earned me a wonderful privilege. Only 10 students out of all the 4th and 5th graders at my school are given this opportunity each year. Everyone tells me I am doing a great job with the news. I now have a better reputation and am learning even more skills. This proves that achieving goals could give you a great unexpected opportunity that could make other dreams of yours come true.

You are Never Too Young to Set Goals

You should also set goals even though you might still be a kid because it helps you make better choices and keep your behavior under control. Let's say you see kids doing things they are not supposed to do. It looks like fun and you are tempted to join in, at the same time, you know that doing this will destroy your goal to have good behavior and could get you in trouble.

Because you are thinking about your goal, you choose not to join in, but without this you probably would have joined them.

Many young people are kicked out of school, on drugs, locked up in juvenile detention or in trouble because of the choices they made. This is why setting goals is important; it helps you think about and plan for your future.

Summary:

A goal is a dream with a deadline.
Achieving goals is the path to a great life.
Goals help you know where you are going.
Goals make you stronger and more capable.
Goals create better opportunities.
Goals help you make better choices.

How to Set Goals

Know Your Strengths

When you are setting goals, you must recognize your strengths and weaknesses. If you are honest with yourself about how good you already are when it comes to your goal, this will help you set better goals. Let me explain:

Let's say you don't like reading much, and are not a fast reader and so you decide to set a goal to become a better reader. The fact that you already know you are not a great reader should help you figure out just how high your reading goal should be.

Your current reading level should tell you not to set a goal too hard for yourself that you might not be able to accomplish. You also want your goal to be challenging or you won't grow.

For example, if you struggle to read 10 pages in a week, don't set a goal to read 100 pages a day. A goal that huge would be unrealistic and you will probably quit. You shouldn't set a goal for just one page a day either. A goal that small is uninspiring and you may end up not even doing that.

Setting unrealistic goals could make you lose hope in yourself and then you'll go back to your old ways. So many people set goals, don't achieve them and set them over and over again and after a while they lose hope that they can ever succeed at that goal.

It's such a waste of time and energy to set yourself up for failure by not setting smart goals. So, don't set a goal to immediately start reading 100 pages a day if you are not that good of a reader.

I have set a challenging goal to read 100 pages a day. It is realistic for me because I have grown up with books and could read very well by the time I was 5 years old.

If you are not in the habit of reading a lot, setting a goal to read 200 pages in a month is more realistic. You can begin with 10 pages each day for a month and see how it works for you. We will talk more about this later in the book.

Choose Your Own Goals

I will also encourage you not to make your goals based on others' opinions. Why? You know more about yourself than anyone. Sure, it's alright to listen to others' opinion but you should stay focused on what you believe you can do even if others don't agree.

Your goals should be based on the dreams you have in your heart for your life.

Here is an example:

When I told my Mom about my goal to read 100 pages a day, she didn't think it was a realistic goal and she encouraged me to lower it. She didn't want me to stress myself out because I am also involved in other activities. I was sure I could meet that goal daily without being stressed because I love to read and I am a fast reader. I decided to keep my goal and I have been reading no less than 100 pages a day, even on weekends.

If I had taken my mother's advice to lower my goal, I wouldn't have the most points from taking Accelerated Reader tests in my entire school. I learn a lot of information from the books I read and this is helping expand my knowledge and vision. I didn't listen to what my mom said about lowering my goal, and I feel more and more successful. Choose your own goal and follow through. However, BE SURE TO RESPECT YOUR PARENTS!

Know What You Want and Why

To be successful, it is not enough to just know your current talents and abilities, you need to take the time to figure out and know what you want. Stop saying, 'I don't know,' when people ask what you want. Start asking yourself daily, 'What do I want?' Take time to answer the question. What do you want now? It doesn't matter how young you are, you should start dreaming big and planning now.

To achieve your goal, you need to know what you want, why you want it and why it is important to YOU. Your goal may be important to others, but you must know why it is important to YOU. Why am I emphasizing this point? If you set a goal, there will be challenges and you may be tempted to quit because it feels like it is too hard. If you set a goal because someone told you to, but that goal does not mean a lot to you, you are more likely to quit.

On the other hand, if you set a goal based on what is important to you, you will try harder than if it was for someone else. Someone else's reasons may be good, but if you have your own reasons for your goal, you will stay more focused. In addition, if you set your own goals, you will build your self-confidence. But, if you base your goals on someone else, then somebody else is always choosing what your life should be. Here is an example:

My mom always encourages us to read so we can improve our vocabulary and be better educated. She also knows that I could qualify for the end-of-year party my principal has for the best readers in the school.

I decided to set the goal of reading 100 pages daily, but I do it because I want to be a better reader and I want to encourage all kids to shine in their own way. My parents do not have to remind me to read to achieve my goal, because I motivate myself and track my own progress. I have no doubt that I will qualify to attend the principal's party based on my effort.

Your goal might help you become a writer or speaker, a better gymnast, or a great math student. It might lead you in the future to take a test for talented students that could open doors for scholarships.

Setting and achieving goals can improve your reputation. At my school, teachers are always looking for students they can depend on. You may be asked to assist a teacher because you are trustworthy and listen well.

You may be the person who gets called to assist another student from your class who doesn't quite understand the concept. Either way, setting goals puts you in a position to help others even as you grow and achieve. This is why you set a goal. Your goals should make you a smarter, stronger and better person. Set goals.

Choose to be excellent. Choose to shine.

Summary:

Know how good you are.
Know what you want.
Know why you want your goal and why it is important to you.
Think for yourself.
Don't let others cause you to shrink or give up on your goals.

How to Stay Focused on Your Goals

Write Your Goals

If you want to be successful at your goal, you need to write it down. When I take the time to write my goals, I become more focused. It is no longer a dream; it is now something that is real that I am going to work on accomplishing.

When you write down a goal it causes you to ask yourself if you are serious or just dreaming. I think many people say they want something, but they are just talking.

Writing down your goal means that even when you get distracted, you can always go back and look at what you've written and remind yourself of what you should be doing.

In my family, we create Vision Boards. We write down our specific goals for the year. Our parents encourage us to dream big and commit to our goals. I have noticed that if I write the goal and put it up, I am focused. When I don't write down the goal, or I write it down and lose it, I don't stay as focused and so I don't achieve it.

Create a Schedule

To achieve a goal, you also need a schedule. If you don't decide when you are actually going to do something, you may never get around to it. Since you are still a kid, you will need to know not only your schedule, but your family's schedule too. This will help you figure out what times you have available to work on your goal. What if the family's schedule is like this one?

3:00 – 3:20 p.m.   Library

3:25 – 4:20 p.m.
  Homework/Reading Time/Playtime

4:30 - 5:30 p.m.   Tennis

  Also, 4:30 – 6:30 sister's dance practice (maybe could read then)

  6:45 – 7:00 p.m.   Finish
homework/Reading Time/Playtime

7:00 - 7:30 p.m.   Dinner

  7:30 - 8:20 p.m.
  Devotional/Bedtime Rituals

  8:20 – 8:30 p.m.   Read in bed

Based on this schedule, if you have decided to read 200 pages a month, how many pages could you read each day? I would say at least 10 pages which will get you over 200 pages even if you miss a day or two.

Looking at the schedule I shared, you will have approximately an hour and forty five minutes, not including the time that is written in italics. If in your family schedule you don't get a lot of time for your goal, work on fitting it in whenever possible or even talk to your parents to see how they can make changes to help you reach your goal.

This does not mean you don't take time to play, it just means that you carve out some time to work towards your goal. What if you had a tight schedule and only had 30 minutes spare time? Use at least half of those minutes to work on your goal.

I play, watch TV, take dance and tennis lessons and I love having fun. But, I also try to use as much free time as possible to read, no matter how small. I read in the bathroom, in the car, and even at school when I finish with an assignment. Don't rush through your assignments, but if you get done with time to spare, use the time to work on your goal.

I know how some of you might feel having to tag along when your parents take others places. We are a pretty active family so someone always needs to be taken somewhere. We are involved in football, tennis, dance, church, basketball, soccer, golf and that makes for a lot of driving. To reach my reading goal, I almost always have a book with me so I can read wherever I may be.

Next, you need to write every possible reason for your goals on a piece of paper. Write why YOU made this goal. What do you think will happen when you achieve your goal? How are you going to stay focused and how will it help you? Have multiple copies of your goal and your reason for setting the goal. You can put the copies in multiple places like your room, your desk at school and if you split time at another home, have a copy there too.

Identify Your Encouragers

The people we hang around can influence us to make good or poor choices. You need to have people who are positive and will encourage you if you are discouraged about your progress. You can also include who you will seek out for encouragement on your goal paper.

You could put something like Mom, Dad, Makayla and Martina will encourage me. If you get discouraged, instead of doubting yourself, you can talk to them and they can lift your spirits. If your parents are really encouraging, they may even reward you as you achieve your daily goal.

Your list could look like this:

Goal: My goal is to go to the party for kids who read 200 pages a month.

Why?: Achieving this goal will make me a better reader, a better student and prove that I can shine and I want to go to the party.

What will happen when I achieve the goal?: I will have become a better reader and will qualify to attend the party.

How will I keep my schedule?: I will spend half my spare time reading wherever I am.

How will this help me in the present or future?: In the present, it could make me an excellent student and one of the most dependable students in the entire class and even in the school. It will also show I am a very capable person. In the future, this might get me into selective programs in middle school and high school and I may even have the option of skipping a grade.

My Encouragers: Mom, Dad, Makayla and Martina

How to stay focused on your goal:
I will stay focused on my goal by following a written schedule, writing down everything that could encourage me on paper, disciplining myself and reaching out to positive people who will reward me when I achieve my goal.

I guarantee each of these will help you stay focused. Write down your goal and make a schedule.

Summary:

Write down your goal.
Make a written schedule.
Identify people who will encourage you.
Write down the benefits of achieving your goal.

How to Respond if You Don't Achieve Your Goal

Don't Quit

Here is a quote that has proved helpful to me when I haven't achieved a goal:

If at first you

don't succeed,

try, try, try again.

It is important to understand that lots of people who are famous now have failed to achieve some of their goals too. Did you know that overcoming our failures actually makes us stronger?

The reason we get stronger if we don't quit, is because our mind begins to say, "I am better than this. I CAN do this. I CAN do this." And since our minds are so powerful, the more we say this, the more creative and stronger we become to push to achieve our goals.

This strength is not automatic. It only comes if you push away your unhappiness about not achieving your goal and focus on moving forward. It is alright if you are sad for a while, but you can't dwell on your lack of success too long or you'll eventually give up hope.

You can be unhappy for a few days, but then you have to let it go. You want to start training your mind to bounce back from negative things quickly by searching for the positive in every situation.

Don't expect your mind to just get those positive thoughts, you have to believe, you have to tell it to think that way. YOU are the key to lifting yourself up. You can do it because you know and understand yourself.

For instance, Abraham Lincoln had to try twice before he was elected president. Today, he is celebrated as one of the most effective presidents the United States of America has ever had. He is on our money and also has a monument in Washington D.C. So, don't give up and don't think badly about yourself. Find ways to keep yourself uplifted and focused on your future not on the mistakes in your past.

Use Affirmations

One way to train your mind to be positive is to use affirmations. Using affirmations is like downloading an application to your phone, iPad or computer. Once you download the application, the device is able to function differently.

Affirmations are simply positive statements that you say to yourself, about yourself and your goals. To be effective, you have to say your affirmations over and over again until you believe them and start to function with that new mindset. Your affirmations should be short and powerful statements.

My siblings and I have been saying the same affirmations for a few years now, and I also make up my own from time to time. Here is the daily affirmation we say on our way to school:

**I am a child of God
I do all things in love
I am the head and not the tail
I know the difference between right and wrong and
I have the courage to do what is right
I can do all things through Christ who strengthens me
And today I am having a phenomenal day!**

Sometimes when I am feeling down, parts of these affirmations will play in my head and I will perk up and remember that I have what it takes to turn things around. Try writing your own affirmation or borrow mine. The more you say them, the more you will believe in yourself and be able to bounce back from failures.

Learn from Your Mistakes

Now, some people are afraid to set goals because they don't want to make a mistake. They don't want to be known as a failure so they just don't set goals. It is okay to make mistakes when you are setting goals. I believe everyone reading this book is capable of making great goals and achieving them. But we ALL make mistakes sometimes and we have to learn to live with that and not allow the fear of making mistakes keep us from trying to be better people.

I am certain that everyone has made a few mistakes regarding setting and achieving their goals. I think most of our mistakes are based on either being afraid of failing or because we got over confident. Yes, over confident.

When people get over confident about their goal, they stop paying attention to the specific things they need to do and think everything will just fall into place. When people are over confident and fail, it is really hard for them to bring themselves back up. Some of those people never rebuild their confidence after a failure and they end up living far below their capabilities.

For those for whom it takes a long time to get over things, wait until you have calmed down before you try to rebuild yourself. Trust me, if you try to rebuild yourself while you are still very sad, you will be fighting yourself, which can get frustrating and tiring. This might get you so tired and frustrated that you quit on yourself.

Once you have rebuilt yourself by remembering your strengths, retrace your steps and find your mistakes. Let's say you only read 150 pages that month, and your goal was 200 pages. You need to find out why you only read 150 pages that month.

Be honest with yourself. Did you stick to your schedule? What, if anything, distracted you? Is the goal unrealistic for you? Maybe you were sick. Whatever the reason, figure out what went wrong and create a plan to avoid those same mistakes in the future.

Thomas Edison estimated that he tried 10,000 times before he invented the light bulb. This is what he had to say about his failures, "I have not failed. I've just found 10,000 ways that won't work. Our greatest weakness lies in giving up. The most certain way to succeed is always to try just one more time." If Thomas Edison can learn from his mistakes and not quit, so can you.

Summary:

Don't be afraid of making mistakes
Learn from your mistakes
Use affirmations to build yourself up
Try, try, try again

We all have one life to live. What we do with our life and our talents is up to us. Those who set and begin achieving their goals at a young age will definitely have very bright futures.

It is time for us kids to shine, shine, shine.

For more information on Kosi Eneli and to book her to speak at your event, visit www.ayaeneli.com, send an email to info@ayaeneli.com or write: Kaneli International Inc. P. O. Box 2789, Harker Heights, TX 76548